From

Pre-Menstrual Syndrome (PMS)

to

Positive Mental Attitude (PMA)

- A Change Management
Guide for Women (and their Men)

Nola Anne Hennessy

Serenidad® Consulting

This book may be ordered through booksellers or by contacting the publisher:

Serenidad Consulting Pty Ltd
PO Box 881
Sanctuary Cove QLD 4212
Australia

Ph: +61 7 55148077
Fax: +61 7 55148088
Email: enquiry@serenidadconsulting.com
www.serenidadconsulting.com

ISBN: 978-0-9874599-3-0 (sc)
ISBN: 978-0-9874599-4-7 (hc)
ISBN: 978-0-9874599-5-4 (e)

US Library of Congress Control Number: 2012904119

Australian National Library CIP - Dewey Number: 158.1

The views expressed in this work are those of the author and the women with whom she has consulted for the case studies. The author does not dispense medical advice or prescribe the use of any technique as a form of treatment for a physical, emotional or mental condition and advises that a qualified physician must be consulted by the reader under those circumstances. The intent of the author is only to offer information of a general nature to help you in your quest for holistic well-being. In the event you use any of the information in this book for yourself, which is your constitutional right, the author and the publisher assume no responsibility for your actions.

Printed in the United States of America

Cover Design by Fineline Advertising, New Jersey USA

Serenidad Consulting Pty Ltd - revision date 10/18/2016

CONTENTS

From Pre-Menstrual Syndrome to Positive Mental Attitude

DEDICATION

This book is dedicated to my precious son Nick.
Had it not been for his miraculous birth, against all the odds, I would
never have experienced the magic and wonder of motherhood, learned
about the positive outcomes that come from truly nurturing another
human being, and learned the true meaning of selfless love.

ACKNOWLEDGMENTS

The people listed below, and also the ladies who remain nameless, deserve special recognition as having provided constructive comments and contributions to this work. They have helped me to focus its content, provide case study participants or data, and/or simply supported me with constructive critique/opinion so that maximum possible value can be drawn by the reader.

Michelle Meadows
Kim Patterson
Tanya Hempshall
Monica Chetty
Vivian Sipsas

I gratefully accept your priceless gifts and willingness to help our world achieve greater understanding. Thank you all. Your input is very much appreciated.

AUTHOR'S SPECIAL NOTE

From Pre-Menstrual Syndrome (PMS) to Positive Mental Attitude (PMA) (in short, *From PMS to PMA*) is the sequel book to *No Boxing Allowed*.

——————⁓⁓∘⌒⊙⌒⊙⌒⌒⊙∘⁓⁓——————

When I was originally planning the content and tone of my future literary works, back in 2004 I thought to write this one first. What became clear to me when I prepared the outlines for my first three books was that *No Boxing Allowed* had to set the style, pace, tone and healing power for all future works. Hence my focus went to that.

At Easter time in 2009 a few key decisions were made about how this book could be written and best serve the outcomes I was seeking. The most important consideration was the lack of time that people have to read books. I have thus aimed to make this book as short as possible, plus easy to reference and read.

I do recommend that you read *No Boxing Allowed* first, for that will enable you to receive the greatest possible benefit from this book. Content from *No Boxing Allowed* is not repeated here simply for the purpose of filling white space and I'll point you to *No Boxing Allowed* whenever necessary to emphasize topics or reinforce understanding.

This book, *From PMS to PMA,* is more than simply a guide. It's my special gift to you. I've exposed myself in this work to enable the deep self-healing and empowerment of women and men around the globe. I want our world to be one where honesty, integrity, trust, giving, caring and compassion are common place, not rare. I want to see every woman and man understand that we really are all walking down the same path – a path to the future – with every step, with every breath. How rocky or smooth that path becomes is largely dependent on our choices - our attitudes, behaviors, actions and words. What we say and do matters equally with what we *don't* say and do.

What we do and don't do is what really defines who we are as human beings. That is what makes us special and unique, and that is how our life journey will be measured for its quality.

———⁓⁓⦵⦵———

HELP ME MAKE THE WORLD
A BETTER PLACE
BY TAKING UP THIS CHALLENGE

———⁓⁓⦵⦵———

October 18, 2016

INTRODUCTION

In early 2002 an extraordinary sequence of events began in my life. That sequence of events started me on a path – one that, intuitively, I knew was the path for the remainder of my physical life.

I knew I had to keep walking steadily forward, no matter what. At times my journey on that path has been way beyond any comprehension of the word challenging and upsetting. It has been a profound awakening in every realm – spiritual, emotional, mental and physical. At times I wanted to give up completely. But I didn't.

I also knew that one day, when the time was right, I'd share that journey with others in order to teach my fellow humans a refreshed approach to living and relationships. I knew I had to put myself out there in the public domain in order to say "Don't make excuses anymore!", because I'm living proof of what I teach in my books and no one can refute the discoveries about PMS and its cure that I articulate here in *From PMS to PMA.*

In my inaugural self-help and inspirational book *No Boxing Allowed,* the reader is taken on a journey of discovery and empowerment. I recount in that book many of my personal life experiences and lessons learned, my observations of and experiences with others, but most importantly I share some details of the sequence of events that began in 2002 and outline how my unique experience can be applied in principle to the reader's own life journey of choices. *No Boxing Allowed* therefore provides the solid foundation for the reader in understanding this book's teachings to a greater and more easily discernible depth.

From PMS to PMA is a compassionate and easy-to-read Change Management Guide for Women and Their Men. It is written as a handy, quick-reference text in language that the reader can understand without having to apply laborious analysis. It does not contain unproven theory, assumptions, or seek to be a purely academic reference. This is a 'why to' and 'how to' reference book that delivers truth through example. Its teachings come as a direct result of the unique and miraculous sequence of events described above and I'm now in a position to share with you and help you on your path to what I can only describe as *bliss.*

In *From PMS to PMA* I've chosen to use the terms women and ladies throughout to refer collectively to the female gender, rather than make an unnecessary and irrelevant distinction between girls and women based simply on chronological age. The major reason for this choice is because the symptomatology often used to label or box women as 'pre-menstrual' can be experienced by all females at any age. You will discover why this is so in the following chapters and in your reflections of *No Boxing Allowed.*

Put simply ladies, *From PMS to PMA* offers you a very bright light at the end of what many of you (and your loved ones) know can be a dark, confusing, suffocating and forbidding tunnel. There are absolutely no excuses anymore to be a bitch, to ostracize and reject your loved ones using 'PMS' as the reason, or to weather the storm of 'pre-menstrual symptoms' alone, or to hide behind the label of 'PMS' and use that as your whip to get what you want, and/or to be cynical and negative about your hormones and how to manage them at a physiological level.

I do not presume that your man will be the best one to help you start your healing and changing journey. Perhaps someone separate from your inner sanctum will be. Perhaps you need to choose a professionally trained and experienced facilitator, and then follow that up by gaining ongoing support from your man. It is important that you trust yourself to recognize, deep inside, whom that best person will be.

And for you gentlemen? Well this is your very bright light in finding peace and harmony in your relationships with women of all ages. It's your key to really understanding the root cause of 'PMS'. But most importantly this is your opportunity to help your women to make right what is clearly wrong, to heal to the best of their ability, and also to heal and empower yourselves. By doing so you will open your eyes and heart to a whole new way of living and relating.

'PMS', like all women's health challenges, is not *secret women's business* to be ignored, whispered about or laughed at, and I encourage you to kindly and compassionately challenge your women-folk if they become complacent about healing and changing for the better.

Only mutually beneficial outcomes will be realized in applying these teachings. Everyone is in a WIN/WIN situation here. Everyone is offered an opportunity to heal from past pain and to gain a much greater understanding that what we have, for centuries, been programmed to believe about PMS is now a thing of the past.

PART 1

It's So Much More Than PMS

CHAPTER 1

The Author's Reality Check - Almost Blinded By The Light

I could begin this chapter by listing the dozens of justifications for why I, as a human being and a woman, could choose to wallow in self-pity and pain. I have had a life punctuated with deep and traumatic loss (my own offspring and also step-children); emotional, mental and physical abuse at the hands of both family and some of the not-so-nice men I chose to be saddled with for a time; supreme levels of betrayal by people who could only be described as having hurtful, destructive and completely selfish intentions; and complete and total abandonment by some of the most important people in my life. As a result of my physical life journey[1] I am, therefore, enormously resilient and strong.

But to articulate my physical life journey and dissect it in minute detail, what good would that do? Well, none really - as all that would accomplish is causing or potentially causing *other* people a great deal of embarrassment, career damage, public ridicule and humiliation. That is not my goal in writing this book.

What I do for you in this book is enlighten you to a different approach to dealing with one of the biggest challenges facing women and men of all ages; and a simple and effective way to change that approach permanently. By simply regurgitating life experiences through this medium, without care for the impact on others, I believe there would be way too much negative fallout and what you would read about would

---

[1] noting that I am on my second spiritual journey in this one physical lifetime

place you in a negative mind space for quite a long time. By revealing too much it could also expose the lives of people with whom I have no further contact. A negative space is not where I want you to be. I want you to focus on the positive things to come.

So, by revealing *just* enough of my personal journey in *From PMS to PMA* it will help you to understand that either your life has been pretty sweet by comparison or that I have known a similar pain to what you are currently going through. Something good *always* comes out of the worst adversity. That is the positive flow-on effect we will achieve, with your equal focus and attention on what is written.

From PMS to PMA will also not betray confidences entrusted to me over time, so I share only that which I consider necessary for you to gain an appreciation of the background to key issues I raise here and in later chapters. Truth is always best, but it must never seek to be destructive. There must always be an undercurrent of compassion and care in revealing truths. My truths are here for you to apply, in principle form, to your own life.

———— ᘒᘖᘓ∘ᗆᘓᘉᘇᘌᘎᘇᘒᘖᘌᘉᘒᘖᘍᘇ∘∘ᘒᘖ ————

No Boxing Allowed was first released globally in August 2009 however I take this opportunity to reinforce one of its key teachings – allow time to pass and the best possible solution to be revealed.

As I journeyed through the emotional exfoliation and deep soul-level healing I describe in *No Boxing Allowed* there were several lightning-bolt revelations during that initial 3 week period and the 9 months that immediately followed. The revelations have cemented my thinking over time:

- that each person will subconsciously process memories and the pain associated, in their own unique way and it takes *time* to work out what way is best for you (see below for a few simple examples);
- the speed at which painful events are processed in the mind is directly linked to a person's state of overall health and the level of nutrients delivered to the brain;
- we must take *real* care how we utilize and channel our positive personal power towards and around others;

4

- we must advocate for and practice positivity in every aspect of our lives, in order for our world and its place in the universe to change for the better, permanently;
- we are given life and opportunities for a reason – to make a positive mark on our loved ones, to nurture relationships (not destroy them), to help our fellow humans whenever and wherever humanly possible – and, by so doing, contribute positively to humanity and the universe; and
- we have to choose who we heal with and for, and who can help us to heal, *very carefully*. If you choose to employ a facilitator to assist you to start your healing journey[2] (e.g. natural/remedial therapist, counselor, psychologist, hypnotherapist) interview or consult with them first. Their true motivations must be *very* easy to discern during that initial dialogue with them. So, if you sense they are not sincere or selfless in their motives to help you, then find someone else.

Apart from the learnings and awakenings listed above, what it took me a few years to check, double-check, triple-check and then accept as a *true miracle* was:

- the 'PMS' symptoms I had experienced all my life literally *vanished* after exfoliation of my emotional pain (my baggage), my estrogen levels soared to an all time high and have remained much higher than expected (medically-speaking for my age group) since. In addition to these wonderful and rejuvenating experiences, my menstrual cycle then came regularly, each 28 days like clockwork; I actually lost most of the lines (wrinkles you could call them) on my face – hence people remark about how I look much younger than my chronological years; my skin became naturally more radiant; the irises of my eyes became ultra clear and unmarked; hearing, taste, smell, sight and touch sensory input increased beyond all comprehension (e.g. no longer needing spectacles to discern things at long distances and only sometimes needing them for close work); and the ability to easily retain new and essential memories became greatly enhanced.

I talk in the first dot point above about subconscious processing of memories and the pain associated. Put simply, when you know you are

---

[2] given that *you* are ultimately responsible and accountable to manage your personal journey using very strong self-motivation

hanging onto 'stuff', *you* have the ability to make a conscious decision to process memories and let go of the pain associated with that 'stuff'.

For instance, you can use imagery to help in visualizing the process of letting go and healing. When you close your eyes and create an image in your mind's eye of 'letting go' (e.g. tearing out the pages of a book or magazine and letting them fall to the floor; or carrying a bag of pebbles and dropping one pebble at a time onto the ground until they're all gone; or sending your pain up to each cloud that floats by), you are then able to *consciously* control the way your mind *subconciously* processes out the baggage associated with memories. And, over time, that technique will be re-programmed into your subconscious permanently - the *subconscious* 'letting go' process will be automatic, triggered by the *conscious* thought process that precedes it. I explain this aspect of personal healing in more detail in Part 2.

───── ༄◦ଓ᳓ᷮᑯᘉᝍᑲ᳚ᑯᷮᘉᵕᝍ◦ᑯ᳚ᵕ᳚᠊ᵕᑯᷮ᠊ᵕᵕᝍᵕᑯᵕᑯᵕᵕᵕᵕᵕᵕ ─────

Under hypnosis the speed of subconscious processing is profoundly increased but with that effect can come the 'too much too soon' scenario, so be careful when choosing hypnosis as the facilitation method. Hypnosis is just one of the many methods to affect deep healing, and the changing of habits and thought processes.

Whilst the most profoundly effective and sustainable method for me was and is positive inner dialogue, other examples are given in *No Boxing Allowed* and I encourage you to find the method that is best for you. Facilitated hypnosis and self-hypnosis can be very confronting for people – you will go over old memories at some stage during that journey in the subconscious realm. And only *some* people will allow themselves to be susceptible to hypnotic suggestion (i.e. a hypnotherapist cannot make you do something you wouldn't consciously choose to do); and only *some* people will allow themselves to journey to a trance-like where deep healing can then occur more rapidly.

However, you must remain forever confident, that the *right method for you* will be the one you discover over time. It will be the method that feels most comfortable to repeat for a positive outcome, as necessary, throughout your life.

The stronger your mind the less likely you are to be influenced by others to maintain negative behaviors and mindsets; the less likely their negative impact will be on you as time progresses.

Mental strength is also directly linked to physical strength. The mind-over-matter (mind-body connection) principle will apply, within your physiological limits placed on you by your body's structure and integrity of course. That is why humans can empower their body's musculature to lift great weights when necessary. The natural instinct to survive and thrive is demonstrated every time we see someone exhibit great strength of mind and body to help themselves or others in times of greatest need.

Now let's look at the 'PMS' aspects as they relate to my own experience:

When I was in my late teens and early 20's I experienced only mild 'PMS' symptoms – a low back ache or feeling of heaviness, temporary weight gain for 1-2 weeks, breast tenderness, and significant pain and cramping during some but not all menstrual cycles. I also suffered headaches at some stage during the menstrual cycle and during most months. My cycle was pretty much a 28-day cycle and I only used contraception for some of those years when I was sexually active and needed to protect myself. My body worked quite well on its own in those teen and early adult years, but the symptoms I believed to be 'PMS'-related became a real drag – they interfered with my love life and social life. I wanted to be free of those burdens.

At 23 I had to undergo two medical procedures in the USA that severely traumatized by body's reproductive system (and my heart) and it was from that date in April 1982 through to March 2002 (20 years later) that I experienced the worst symptoms of all. My cycle became unpredictable, menstruation became very heavy at times (the term women often use is flooding) and then by age 34 I had all the symptoms of and was diagnosed by my gynecologist as going through early-onset menopause. At that time my estrogen levels were found to be way too low, from what the medical fraternity called normal for my age group, so I commenced Hormone Replacement Therapy (HRT).

HRT was great while I was taking the estrogen supplements, in fact it was almost blissful, but as soon as I went onto the progesterone, to facilitate a period, I felt like killing all the people I was unhappy with (including my then husband) on sight. I'd suffer temper outbursts following continual provocation from others (their behavior triggering my reaction) and mood swings[3] that *seemed* totally uncontrollable. What I mean by that is I *chose* to have the emotional reactions to other people's behavior and actions. I didn't realize at the time that the symptoms I was

---

[3] where I'd be in tears prior to each period, feeling unloved and unsupported

experiencing were not really related to hormonal changes, they were related to the emotional health of my relationships with others.

It took only a few weeks (6 in fact) to realize that HRT was a toxic remedy for the symptoms and so-called pre-menopausal phase. HRT was actually exacerbating the impact of my emotional baggage – the unresolved painful memories – which I hadn't yet recognized as being the root cause of the 'PMS' symptoms. HRT was only *managing* some of the hormonal aspects, not getting to the root cause. I decided there had to be another way.

My then marriage suffered much more during these few HRT weeks than it ever had previously. There'd been some very painful experiences that my then husband and I had journeyed through together and that had, to some extent, brought us much closer emotionally. But it wasn't the fact that I was managing symptoms all the time, it was more that I felt trapped in a marriage where I didn't want to be and had a whole lot of deep-seated pain from that and previous relationships [4] that needed to be resolved. HRT was just complicating the already unmanageable emotional foundation for the 'PMS' symptoms.

People have always described me as being pretty laid back, unflappable etc. and, during that hardest time, even though I was experiencing negative physical symptoms I remained 'laid back' to the most part. I presented to the world in the same manner privately as I did publicly, a trait that stays with me today, i.e. I'm the same in my style, attitudes and behavior regardless of the type or level of scrutiny and exposure. But what I was feeling on the inside, at times during HRT and the pre-menopausal period of time, was obviously not manifesting quite so openly on the outside for the majority to see; in hindsight, this was a good thing.

I've also always had a foundation positive mindset and chosen to be as nice as possible under difficult circumstances, but when pushed and pushed by others' bad behavior or non-supportiveness; when feeling controlled and suffocated by others' expectations of me and the desire to keep me (quite selfishly) 'all to themselves' and not share me with others; or when others have not allowrf me the freedom to express myself, I'd always retaliate with either frustration or annoyance. For a period of about 4 years during my 30's, not at all linked to my menstrual cycle, the annoyance and frustration would sometimes manifest as anger outbursts. Whilst I would say loudly to people "get out", "go away" or "stop". I felt

---

[4] including relationships with other men, family and friends

that anger more and more each time on the inside. I felt like a time bomb waiting to go off. That was the worst time of my life, wondering how to break free so that I could heal properly.

So what was I really angry about? Well, apart from being supremely frustrated at all the above attempts to control and manipulate an outcome I didn't want, I was also upset and in pain at the people I despised for having deliberately chosen to hurt me, and those I loved and cared about, by their selfishness, dishonesty, cruelty, ego-centered approach to life, profound arrogance, laziness and cynicism.

I knew something had to give at some stage, but I didn't want that something to be my health. At the same time I was undergoing HRT, experiencing the worst symptoms of all time, I was also in a state of inner mental conflict – I couldn't find definitive answers to long-held questions or identify workable solutions to remove some of my worst relationship challenges. Within months I was diagnosed as being pre-cancerous (at a cellular activity level). That was the loudest awakening for me at that time – I knew I had to resolve the inner conflict (which I strongly believe is a causal factor for cancer), and clear the painful thoughts in my head, in order not to have a serious illness manifest itself in my body at some future time.

I ceased the HRT really swiftly and for a couple of years that followed I underwent the chiropractic "Activator" method – a very helpful way for me to free up energetic pathways in my body. I also gained qualifications as a remedial massage therapist and Reiki practitioner and managed to find some time to channel some of that healing power to myself and work on my own chakra points and energy meridians. But, more importantly, I took more regular time out away from the people I found to be toxic in their negative use of personal power. I found I was distancing myself from those I knew would never change (their low self-esteem and lack of confidence were cleverly disguised as arrogance and cruelty in most cases) and whom I knew would continue to have a negative impact on me.

It wasn't until I left my marriage and ceased contact with other toxic people and underwent the deep healing that I describe above and in *No Boxing Allowed,* that I achieved a permanent cure from decades of so-called 'PMS' symptoms. I have, with less than a handful of exceptions, had a life of absolute bliss ever since. Sure, I've experienced disappointment and hurt, grieved people who have died or are no longer a part of my life, but in reality I've lived a whole new life since 2002 thanks to the deep soul-level cleansing and exploration.

I don't carry pain for longer than ½-2 weeks at the very most, ever. I feel disappointed, upset or saddened by events from time to time, but holding onto the emotional pain associated with memories (i.e. the baggage) is something my mind is no longer capable of doing. I have programmed my subconscious mind to process memories over and over until the pain (that has originated in my heart) is gone. If what I see or hear triggers a painful response and a memory is recalled, I relax through it knowing that I'll come out the other end with total serenity and peace of mind and heart.

Some people, who don't understand how I can recover so quickly from painful events, see me as being superficial in my feelings. Well the complete and total opposite is actually true. I feel things very deeply and have simply developed a method (through necessity and for survival) that allows me not to get *trapped* in the pain associated with deeply painful events I experience. I don't allow pain to control my life and my heart.

I have control over how I recover from events. I don't rely on someone else to take control of helping with how I feel or how long it takes me to heal. I'm responsible for my own happiness and maintaining it. I don't consider it's not a man's responsibility to "make" me happy or likewise my responsibility to help a man get happy and stay happy. The motivation is strongly within me and, quite rightly, I'm relieved and very empowered by my capacity to heal myself, recovering from painful experiences without the need for anyone else's direct involvement.

That capacity to *self-heal* is within everyone, given the correct support mechanisms and structures. The skill with which you can achieve ongoing self-healing is also something that's within *your* power to acquire and hone. When you think about the alternative – always looking to someone else to heal you and make things better – you are not using the innate power that is right there, in your soul, to be tapped into 24/7 every day of the year.

The subconscious processing I talk about above occurs most rapidly when I'm asleep but it also continues (even right at this second as I type) through the day. That gift of *emotional exfoliation* is the miraculous gift I gave myself years ago and, given the often times traumatic life I've had to endure through my own and others' choices, that is well and truly my key to expert survival under circumstances that would break most other humans.

By saying this I'm not expressing an arrogance about my ability. Not at all. By my declaring the mind power that I know I possess and the high level of self confidence that comes from knowing myself so well, all I'm doing is reinforcing to you that anything is possible. *You choose how your mind works. You choose the mindset you'll hold each day, the way you process memories, and the mindset you want for the future.*

My mind will not tolerate negative thought processes in any shape or form. It's literally impossible for me to think negative throughts beyond the immediate impact timeframe. And I've used myself as a scientific experiment on many occasions, especially during 2007-2009, to test that very fact. My body responds to any negative thought processes or incoming dialogue from other people very quickly, and in predictable and discernable ways (ways that I recognize through being in tune with my body at all times). For example, when engaged in dialogue with other people, actively listening to others speak, I automatically convert negative words to positive words (see the chart in Part 1, Chapter 6 of *No Boxing Allowed*).

And what that positive mindset helps to reinforce, and feed back to my body, is positive nurturing energy. Someone can say something negative, directed at me personally or about a situation, but my mind automatically reinforces back to the positive so that I don't labor on the negative aspects of what I heard or saw. That positive nurturing energy is the energy that remains ever present, ensuring that I maintain a blissful state where so-called 'PMS' can never resurface.

Granted I'm now near 60 and have long been post-menopausal. The transition through menopause was pretty much uneventful, as I fully expected it to be!

CHAPTER 2

PMS – Symptoms, Myths and Excuses

According to Mosby's Medical, Nursing and Allied Health Dictionary[5], 'PMS' is a syndrome of nervous tension, irritability, weight gain, oedema (fluid retention), headache, mastalgia (breast pain), dysphoria (depression and anguish), and lack of coordination occurring during the last few days of the menstrual cycle just before menstruation begins. Mosby's further explains that there are several theories that attempt to explain the cause of 'PMS' – nutritional deficiency, stress, hormonal imbalance and various emotional disorders.

Other reported symptoms of 'PMS' include radical mood swings, temper outbursts, extreme aggression (in most severe cases), anxiety, food cravings, blood sugar disturbance, tiredness, and the desire to be alone. It is *believed* to be completely linked to ovulation i.e. no ovulation, no 'PMS'.

Common remedial action prescribed for the 'sufferer' includes stress reduction, lifestyle changes, vitamin supplements, exercise, hormone therapy, anti-depressants, diuretic medication, anti-inflammatory drugs, ovarian surgery, the contraceptive pill and even the woman changing her activities to suit 'mood' swings. Some also believe relationship counselling and herbal treatment will minimize symptoms.

When I look at all the above I laugh. **Firstly**, because 'PMS' is the 'label' or 'box' given for a range of symptoms that women can experience *completely unrelated to their menstrual cycle*. For instance,

---

[5] not a criticism of Mosby's overall value at all, just used as a simple reference text

people suffer oedema in their feet if they sit at a desk or table too long or don't elevate their feet or walk around often enough; when they wear little sockets to bed in winter – they have a tight ankle band that limits the lymphatic system's ability to return fluid from extremities; and when they stand for too long in a static position. Breast enlargement can be experienced as a result of feeling deep love for others. In fact my breast size, since the emotional exfoliation journey of years back, has remained 2 cup sizes larger than ever before in my life (quite a bonus as I always wanted bigger boobs!). My increased breast size and comfort I put down to two key things – feeling love for myself much more easily than I ever was capable of before (a direct result of forgiving myself and others), and being able to express love and give love freely to those who willingly want to receive it.

People can experience low back pain when relationships are ending or a new beginning is evident – the physical manifestation of what the mind and heart are going through – the foundations crumbling or forming.

Secondly, because mood changes are related to emotions and emotions are at work 24/7, not just in the latter stages of the menstrual cycle. And, **most importantly**, men have emotions too! Men don't have a menstrual cycle so how can mood swings and mood changes be the realm of existence for women only?

In fact, when you go back and re-read the very first sentence, and then the first sentence of the second paragraph in this chapter you'll see that a man could be labelled as suffering 'PMS' because *he* can experience those same symptoms himself! How many men would tolerate being told "You've got PMS Jack. Sorry, you just have to accept it as a way of life! And, by the way, it'll get worse when you get to change of life!"?

How convenient is it for the medical fraternity to tick the list of symptoms that someone comes to them with, and then say "Oh well, you must have 'xyz' wrong with you."? Simply ticking off the list of symptoms, giving the list a diagnosis 'label' is not resolving the root cause. And, no doubt, many of the treatments that women are prescribed or forced to undertake 'for their own good' are simply an experimental form of medical discovery. Is that why a medical "practice" is so named? I wonder!

The challenge I put to all in the medical fraternity is 'PMS' *need not exist in your text books and medical reference documents*. Also, and most importantly, severe 'PMS' symptoms must *not* be classified a form of mental illness. 'PMS' is not a mental or medical disorder. Its collective symptoms, as they manifest in women and men equally, are a direct result of unresolved pain from memories of past events, often exacerbated by a negative mindset. Nothing more, nothing less. I'm living proof of what can be achieved by a woman and I have absolutely no doubt that if a man underwent the same emotional exfoliation he too would feel bliss at the other end of that journey, and thereafter.

———~~o◦e◦◦◦o◦~~———

Knowing that I don't have to add weight to my own testimony, to justify my findings in any way, I've still chosen to share with you the stories of a sample of case study women who were approached and then actively volunteered to contribute to this book. The women surveyed vary in age from 37 to 52. In every case real names are withheld in order to protect their privacy. Case study numbers are the only identifiers.

Their journeys in life are as unique and special as they are and I'm most grateful for their honesty and candidness in sharing their 'PMS' beliefs and appropriate hormonal/medical histories for your benefit and greater understanding.

Each lady was provided with background information on 'PMS' as documented at the beginning of this chapter. They were asked the same specific set of specially crafted questions but each drew on their own life experience to answer honestly and intelligently in their own words, the way they felt most comfortable. Where I sought greater clarity, further questions were asked of them.

I conducted one group workshop where most of the ladies were able to participate on the nominated day. Those who attended actively and positively contributed to achieving greater understanding of the perceived impact of 'PMS' on both themselves and their significant others.

CASE STUDY 1

Married mother of 3, age 47

This woman states she is happily married with 3 adolescent children. For the most part her life has been happy, though she's experienced some long-standing and underlying health issues. She describes her major life events as having travelled the world for 5 years, marrying, having her family, buying a house, changing career directions and changing jobs every 3 years. At 45 she went through a period of crisis with a life-threatening health event; so serious that she required surgery and needed to "reassess life". Her period stopped at this time (for 4 months).

She says she does get 'PMS' and it manifests as irrational anger outbursts, tension, being upset and insomnia. Her emotions are more intense during this time. Symptoms increase when there is underlying stress to deal with as well. She believes she copes with it, but just before her period the anger becomes more intense and she tends to yell at her family about house chores; she gets overwhelmed with all she has to do, all she has to think about; "so many jobs". She also suffers a bloated abdomen (fluid build-up), wants to eat more and has cravings for sugar.

On the upside she's noticed she's been more relaxed, symptoms seem to have decreased since she stopped having a period while on medication for her medical condition. She believes her temperament has been more even and that this is noticeable to everyone. "I'm nicer" she says.

In identifying the root causes of her 'PMS' she states – tiredness, day-to-day stress in life, too busy (overwhelmed with working full-time, cooking, cleaning, being the taxi driver for the family), poor exercise and unhealthy lifestyle, and having no creative outlet. In more general terms this woman believes 'PMS' is due to:

- partly, the Western woman's lifestyle – women aren't given time to just "be", which is very different to other cultures and in years gone by; women are working as well as running a family and there's no downtime to rest;
- body chemicals and hormones change rapidly, and in some people on a month-by-month basis;
- women not being linked to each other as a social group. There's a culture of individualization, "making women feel unsupported (with) no time to socialise and share";
- families being nuclear and therefore generational support isn't available to share the load of running the home; managing a family is still the woman's primary responsibility;
- chemicals in food leading to poor quality food which then causes sluggish bodies;
- not enough exercise;

- having no creative outlet; and/or
- women not being in touch with their bodies and emotions.

She believes that 'PMS' happens, and increases, when all these factors are present or out of balance.

In managing her own symptoms this woman does take some exercise, goes to bed early and has time on her own where being quiet helps her to center herself. She uses music to calm, drinks extra water and eats a healthier diet of food (with regular food intake, given that hunger increases her tension). She defers making decisions to another time and when she feels more relaxed she talks with her family about the annoying challenges of running a household of 5. To ensure positive remedial outcomes this woman works to:

- give herself permission to look after herself by having some rest;
- plan ahead with things where possible;
- provide a creative outlet for herself that reduces tension and gives her a sense of achievement; and
- make healthy lifestyle choices (diet, water, rest) which will give her better general health outcomes.

CASE STUDY 2

Married mother of 2, age 52

This women was born outside Australia, grew up with 3 siblings, but alcohol and domestic violence were quite common in the family household. The children were not physically harmed however the mental pain was, and still is, a part of her life (i.e. what she experienced as a child stays with her as an adult). Her father suffered a trauma and for many years "things were pretty bad".

Even though she first married at 24, she lived and worked elsewhere than Australia until age 30. She is clear in her adoration of her children, both born by caesarean section.

Her marriage was violent, unhappy and controlling. There were no adequate support systems or crisis centers where she lived at that time. After coming to Australia the same violent and drunken behaviors continued and after several intervention orders she and her husband separated and then divorced (she at age 39).

Her children are obviously a great support to her; they are her "great friends". She sees her children as her greatest achievement and the best and only good thing to come of the marriage. After several short and one long relationship she finally met "the man of my dreams" at age 50 and is very happy and quite content with her life.

This woman describes her 'PMS' symptoms as severe bloating, breast tenderness and very severe mood swings a week before her period. She also suffers very bad headaches and stomach cramps. She's been diagnosed with fibroids and endometriosis (sp) and is currently being monitored by a specialist women's health hospital in Australia. For the past few years she's been having 3 periods every 2 months, though the previous time she had a "major issue" was at approximately 29 years of age before she moved to Australia. At that time she suffered severe bleeding. Of late she's had irregular cells discovered after a pap smear but been advised that there's "nothing to worry about".

Medication is avoided except for pain killers when the pain becomes unbearable. Daily doses of fish oil and evening primrose oil are part of her remedial action plan. In managing the changes that have occurred recently, she believes these changes have to do with her age – menopause around the corner, her children grown up, greater freedom in her own life and more disposable income.

When she has spoken with her doctor about the possible cause of 'PMS' they've not been able to come up with anything definitive.

CASE STUDY 3

Married, no children, age 38

This woman has been married for 3 years though with her husband now for a total of 15 years. They don't have children yet and she's "getting a bit worried" about that as the "clock is ticking". She says there's a fine balance between getting her husband to come on board with the idea and "going psycho" herself – this is her major life challenge at this time.

18

Her other challenges in life include her father having serious life threatening health episodes when she was 30 years of age. She feels for her father's situation and also worries about her mum, whom she holds in high regard for having cared so well for her father before he was moved to a nursing home only recently.

Pivotal events in her life so far are meeting her husband when she was 23 and then getting married. She's completed tertiary studies in the health sciences this year and has had her eyes opened to the idea of meditation, and spirituality without religion. She hopes to have children in the future.

This woman has experienced bad period pain since her early 20's and never really thought much of it until her mother alerted her to having suffered the same way during her life. During her mid-late 30's she's been treated for cervical cancer as she had a few irregular pap smears. During the operation her specialist claimed to have "severed the nerve that was giving (her) the pain". She's obviously not impressed that he severed a nerve but she sees her 'body attempting to tell her something but she hasn't quite figured out what that is yet'. Since the operation she's experienced some "massively biiiig periods" with lots of bleeding. There are sometimes 'accidents' due to irregularities and she's discovered, in hindsight, that prior to the last episode she "was NUTS, Grumpy, angry, tired!!"

She's obviously grateful that her husband is a champion for putting up with her, as in the last 5 years she's noticed she gets more emotional before her period – either angry, sooky/weepy, or both. Her focus has been on her health challenges.

In managing the symptoms she experiences, this woman takes pain killers (but only when desperate). She uses a warmed wheat bag for comfort and if she's really lucky she gets a massage from her husband.

Given she and her husband are focused on having children she does more now to monitor her cycle and get more in tune with herself. She sees a naturopath for assistance with her iron deficiency. She also visits a chiropractor for applied kinesiology – this also helps with the monitoring of her hormone levels and helps her to recognize when her 'body is out of whack'. At a personal level she's applying her own learnings with regard to her emotions and hormones. This woman does chakra work on herself.

The positive results she's seen from remedial action include the severed nerve, though this only worked for a time and she gets pain again now. Pain killers work well, but she avoids those wherever possible. Applying warmth is helpful and using her own hand over her abdomen also gives some relief. Warm baths also work well for her as does chocolate when she's feeling sooky and moody. She's experienced some very interesting results from kinesiology and naturopathic work.

In tapping into her emotional side this woman's belief is that emotional stuff is connected to 'PMS' and is a root cause. She recognizes that, for her, there's been a lot of repressed anger in her life, and she acknowledges where this could possibly have its roots. Whilst she has several theories as to what could be causing the 'PMS' at a physical level she just tends to deal with symptoms as they happen and maintains a sense of humor to see her through the worst.

CASE STUDY 4

Married mother of 2, age 37

This woman has been married 14 years and has 2 children under 10 years of age. When she was 31 her father passed away suddenly and unexpectedly. A year ago her husband lost his job so she went back to work full-time and is now the breadwinner in the family. A complete role reversal has occurred in the family.

She often feels lethargic and experiences quite bad mood swings and "stress" just before menstruation. There are cravings for sweet things and she also has temper outbursts.

In managing the symptoms she experiences, she looks to pain killers, does her best to relax and rests more (including having a lie down when she gets home from work). The pain killers afford her immediate results by easing any pain or discomfort. Rest has a medium to long term positive result as it makes her feel calmer and more relaxed. When she 'tunes out' she thinks more clearly.

This woman's belief about the root cause of 'PMS' is that it's closely linked to hormonal changes, and that the physical occurrence of menstruation has an emotional and mental response.

CASE STUDY 5

Married mother of 3, age 50

Now post-menopausal this woman is happily married after 19 years of what she calls the usual ups and downs. She's very satisfied with having had, breast fed and raised her children, and describes herself as a very hands-on parent. The youngest of the children has mild autism which presents its own challenges for child and parents alike. Her experiences in breast feeding the children have given her a different appreciation and understanding of how her body works and how it copes with everyday stressors and she also feels surprisingly content with her post-menopausal stage of life.

Her medical history is not marked with major events, though she believes that prior to menopause she may have been very difficult to live with at times. Herbal remedies, vitamins and mineral supplements were used to regulate her hormonal changes, and to some extent and degree these helped. She also attempted to do more exercise and get enough sleep though an arthritis condition she was suffering (unbeknown to her at the time) was the main root cause of sleep and exercise disturbance. A continual source of ongoing frustration is movement restrictions which have resulted in weight gain over the last 5 years.

During menopause transition, she sought advice from a specialist Women's Center where she was advised that the transitional symptoms were to be expected and that she should go with the flow – some advice she said was the best advice for her at the time.

It is her personal belief that hormones are mighty forces and require respect. The various health reports showing connections between HRT and cancer were enough for her not to go down that path. The root causes of 'PMS' she believes are all to do with keeping a finely tuned balance of naturally occurring hormones. She believes if this can't be done with mild treatments then women need to consider replacements.

CASE STUDY 6

Previously married mother of 2, age 48

Now divorced 13 years after 12 years of marriage and 7 years in a relationship prior to that, this woman is quite happy to be single with two grown children. She's had relationships with 4 other men since divorcing, none of whom she wanted to stay or live with long term. She prefers not to have another adult living in the home with her and her children.

As a major life-changing experience she views her divorce as a combination of choices by other people that impacted adversely on the family unit. She lost trust in her then husband and that's the "saddest" part of the whole experience. In hindsight she has no regrets, despite her marriage being interfered with by another person, a situation she considers immoral. She strongly believes that people should decide to leave a marriage under their own steam, do some soul searching and then consider the next marriage[6].

Travel has been an important contributor to her life, as has her work, and she's maintained lifelong friends in each of her workplaces. Celibacy is a choice and she doesn't "climb the walls" after a few months without sex.

She experiences 'PMS' symptoms (mood mainly) a few days prior to her period and sees this as a result of changing hormones. She's more prone to the odd emotional outburst or tears, and also seeks to eat more during these preceding days. She's been on the contraceptive pill most of her life, with gaps here and there, and thus her hormonal response has been fairly straight forward with no major issues she believes.

Whilst she's not entered menopause she believes that changes are occurring. In managing her symptoms and hormones this woman stopped beating herself up for how she was feeling. She took control, noticed the changes that were happening and made allowances for herself. She altered 'the pill' to fit in with her life, choosing to miss periods when they were possibly going to inconvenience her life.

In terms of root causes she believes that environment does influence a woman's response to 'PMS' e.g. when women and girls grow up with high levels of drama associated with their period and 'PMS' then their suffering may be greater. She considers the event ('PMS' and

---

[6] a view completely agreed with by the author

then later the period) as just that, an event. Whilst she's known of women who suffer greatly and that their symptoms are not "all in their head", she does believe that women sometimes choose to dwell on the negatives way too long and thus their struggle to deal with elements of their life are as a result of being negative thinkers rather than anything else.

———————————

It's interesting to see the obvious differences in all these case studies isn't it? But there are common threads also. 'PMS' is not just a simple set of symptoms, each of the ladies has recognized and dealt with what is happening in their own unique way, and women experience many different symptoms depending on their life histories and coping strategies.

In the group workshop I found the women were more in tune with what impact 'PMS' had on them, with less understanding of the impact on others. Their perceptions of the impact of 'PMS' on their male partner and/or children were the main considerations.

In terms of the most upsetting aspect of 'PMS' on themselves they listed:

o   frustration and lack of acceptance about what was happening in their bodies;
o   inconsistency and unpredictability of their period – they felt dictated to by their hormones;
o   that they can see the patterns in their reactions, mood swings etc. but cannot seem to change – the bitchiness or mood swings seem to just come; they are unplanned;
o   sometimes it's easier to be in denial of changing behaviors – symptoms get worse over time as a result;
o   that, for one, she uses 'PMS' as a venting mechanism for her repressed anger and to maintain her 'victim' mode and mindset;
o   the rawness of emotions during that time of the menstrual cycle makes them more vulnerable to saying things without hesitation (though staying more controlled at work and then letting loose when they get home); and
o   impatience with themselves and others.

———————————

When we looked at why they believed symptoms got worse over time, the following issues were highlighted:

- o symptoms escalate as a result of not venting; not expressing themselves emotionally;
- o body energies being out of alignment can increase the volume of a woman's period and that the root cause of this is emotional;
- o time out isn't available to women due to the speed of life and there's a lack of understanding that women need time to rejuvenate etc.;
- o women suppress their communication because they believe their man is not understanding them and may react in a negative way towards them;
- o hormones are an underestimated driver of life;
- o in some cultures woman veil themselves to reveal to the world that they're ready for marriage and childbearing. This is a controlling aspect of the country's culture and restricts a woman in being able to express herself the way she needs and wants;

  and even

- o women may in fact *accept* that their symptoms are meant to get worse over time.

Whilst impact on themselves was a main focal point I also asked them to look at how their symptoms may be impacting on others. This is the array of opinions expressed, noting of course that this is a very personal and subjective range of comments:

- o some members of the family are supportive and empathetic whilst others don't listen and are very dismissive – having a "get over it" attitude;
- o some male partners seem to ride the storm quite well (though sometimes the husband's good nature can be taken advantage of);
- o one woman knows she uses 'PMS' to be a bitch at home but is completely professional at work; and
- o one husband even experiences sympathy pains and mood changes along with his wife.

Nonetheless, the most fundamental point agreed by all women is that 'PMS' is not really something that's talked about much in society, even in all female households. That's an interesting consensus and may be partly due to the secrecy associated with women's health, a lack of emotional maturity of some people demonstrated in their inability to openly discuss such topics, a general lack of awareness of cause-and-effect, and lack of understanding or appreciation of universal energy and power (explained in more detail in *No Boxing Allowed*).

CHAPTER 3

Trapped With Nowhere To Go? Recognizing the Signs of an Abusive and/or Controlling Relationship

In *No Boxing Allowed* I teach you about recognizing where you are at in life, and if not happy with your findings, how to determine where it is that you want to be and how to get there.

Any empowerment journey will be fulfilling but, in the case of empowering yourself to make change that is directly related to a relationship, it can be a daunting task for many women (and men), especially those who are trapped in unfulfilling, controlling and/or abusive relationships.

So how is this related to 'PMS'? Well, it's my strong belief that many of the challenges that face women (and thus their men) in relationships are based on a control and power imbalance. I also strongly believe that it's this lack of balance that exacerbates a woman's negative emotions which, in turn, can lead to the explosiveness or 'moodiness' seen during the onset of her menstrual cycle.

In other words, there is far more to this journey than just healing yourself from pain, and thus 'PMS'. It's about recognizing and facing the underlying causes, and then working hard to achieve equality and balance of power in the relationship or, in irreconcilable circumstances, ending the relationship altogether.

Whether it's the woman or the man being abusive, controlling, manipulative, suffocating or (in very simple terms) ugly towards the other, it matters not which of the pair initiates positive change, so long as someone does.

In the next Part of this book I take you on that change journey but, for now, let's focus on some root causes.

In my own life I've experienced intimate relationships with men and friendship/family-based relationships with both men and women:

- that have left me feeling completely disempowered to extricate myself from a bad situation;
- where the threat of grave personal harm has been held over my head as a controlling tool;
- where I've been forced to do or say things against my will;
- where I've been publicly ridiculed, slandered, and physically mishandled or assaulted;
- where I've been privately beaten or emotionally abused;
- where I've been wrongly accused, repeatedly; and
- where I've been emotionally isolated, unsupported and/or verbally abused to the point of wanting to end my own life just to achieve a sense of total freedom and control again.

Despite all of these experiences in life I'm blissfully happy, content with my choices, have no regrets[7]; maintain a very strong focus on the future; have forgiven myself for (i) having, in a few cases, chosen to place myself at risk; and (ii) having trusted the people who placed me in harm's way or directly inflicted pain; and have also forgiven others.

One of the most challenging things for me to achieve though, whilst all this was going on, was actual recognition and acceptance that I was in a toxic relationship at the time. We don't often see what is happening to us or with others; we wear rose-colored glasses and are blind to realities; we forgive the wrong-doer(s) but then don't extricate ourselves from the toxic relationship when the same negativity happens again; we keep hoping and wishing that the wrong-doer will change and improve; or we see ourselves as having no power.

I had to start identifying the patterns of behavior and evaluating the impact(s), a bit like causal analysis, before I could see clearly what the flaws in the respective relationships were. Gaining awareness, assessing

---

[7] given that regrets come from non-acceptance of the past, not letting go, retaining blame of self and others, and/or mental confusion about past choices

your findings and deciding a course of action can take years and also not be as easily discernable until you repeat the circumstance with a different person. Sometimes people don't even bother to gain the awareness.

Love is a very powerful and forgiving emotion and you could blindly be journeying on in a relationship that's toxic, without even caring or acknowledging that it is. Love is seen as the cure-all when in fact it's a very controlling emotion, if you let it be. Empowering yourself to understand and accept that you can love someone but choose not to be with them, is enormously helpful when you are forced to make choices. Yet how easy is it for people to stay in their comfort zone, in the cycle and pattern of abuse? It's such a pity when apathy replaces motivation, don't you think?

When I think back to my teens, 20's, 30's and early 40's I must admit I always reached the same point of awareness after observation and engagement – where I believed men and women were pretty much patterned the way society expected them to be. I could see the same relationship scenarios repeating over and over, everywhere I looked and listened. Everything in the media and in movies looked to perpetuate wrong-doing and acceptance of toxic behaviors.

As human beings it's sometimes very challenging to step out of our comfort zone, what we perceive as the safe zone, even if that so-called safe zone is really *un-safe* and is damaging to our wellbeing, as mentioned above. For some of you, stepping out of your comfort zone may seem terrifying, but ultimately the *choice* to place yourself in a fear space (anticipating a negative outcome before a future event has even taken place) is all yours. Fear doesn't have to be the driver for change, nor does fear have to be the vehicle to your destination. Fear is a destructive energy in the body and *No Boxing Allowed* will help you to recognize and grow beyond fear (Part 1, Chapter 8) so that your journey and the changes you choose to make along the way, are founded in positive energy, not negative. I do recommend you read that chapter in *No Boxing Allowed* now, before continuing.

And of course the reality is that many people don't learn lessons from their wrong-doing. They continually make the same mistakes, repeat the same behaviors and their soul doesn't mature and grow better over time. The karmic lessons are ignored. They never change for the better, and in some cases they change for the worse.

Controlling relationships are pretty easy to pick, once you know what you're looking for. Unfortunately the people in the relationship may not see themselves as being either the controller (or puppeteer) or the controllee (the one confined, controlled or disempowered). It's through the perpetual negative energy that controlling behavior generates that we see a positive person – a non-controlling person by nature – themselves become increasingly controlling, or negative and destructive in their soul traits over time. Perhaps they're weak-minded and don't realize the subtle manipulation that they're unwittingly falling victim to. Perhaps they have no desire to take control of their own outcomes, simply want and easy life and to 'go along for the ride', 'cruising' on someone else's efforts. If that's their choice in life, so be it. But, the karmic ramifications on themselves, their loved ones and future generations who continue to practice these negative behaviors without recognizing the patterns and changing things for the better, will be profoundly negative.

Abusive relationships are very different to controlling relationships however, even though there's most likely an element of negative control and disempowerment happening in order for the abuser to remain in the power space. Abusive relationships are usually, but not always, very well hidden by the parties involved. The silence that surrounds abusive relationships is well known, but what's most important for me to convey here (to the people right there in the relationship) are the warning signs that a relationship has become or is becoming destructive, or is dysfunctional in some way. In later chapters I'll provide focused solutions for how you can achieve positive and lasting change and eliminate abuse, control and manipulation from your relationship(s) altogether. But, for now, let's focus on what's wrong and needs to change.

Maintaining silence about abuse can have many root causes:

- it's one of those things that people just "don't talk about" – the ostrich mentality is adopted (head goes in the sand) and everyone hopes it will "all just go away" miraculously by itself;
- people adopt the 'ignorance is bliss' mindset;
- to save face amongst peers, colleagues, family and friends;
- to remove the likelihood of public ridicule or embarrassment;
- to not be seen as having "failed" in a relationship – see the last chapter of *No Boxing Allowed* for more about there being no failures in life; and/or
- to risk manage the likely event that further (and worse) abuse will result from the disclosure of wrong doing.

This last point is probably the most important. From my own experience I've been warned not to speak up or make public what was

30

clearly wrong in a relationship, using the "it's private", "no-one else needs to know", "I don't want (so-and-so) to be hurt", "I'll sue you", "and who's going to care or believe you?", "I'll deny it", "You'll get it worse next time", or even still "So, you're back for more....?" excuses and threats; when clearly I was the one being controlled (at the time) by their selfish, destructive and manipulative intentions.

Societal and peer pressure to maintain appearances of normality, fear of discovery of wrong-doing (and not knowing the outcomes that will come from that), and fear of retribution[8] are all seriously compelling motivators for silence by both parties. But when it all boils down to it, truth will emerge in time regardless of any silence maintained. Truth will come as a lesson, for all parties involved, when you do nothing to change things for the better. How the lesson emerges is unknown to me or you – the karmic lessons we receive come in many forms – so you may not see what's happening at the time. But if you're the one who's being or has been abused, controlled or manipulated and you've done all you possibly can to make things better, then you can be assured the wrong-doer will be brought to justice at some point in their spiritual journey. Even with silence by all parties involved, universal justice will be served when the time is right for their soul to learn the lesson.

———— ∿∿o⌒꙳⌒꙳⌒∽∿∽ ————

So what are some of the key warning signs of a relationship where power is unbalanced, there are abusive undertones or actions, the abuse of a person's position or status is used as a lever to achieve outcomes, and/or where total control is of paramount importance to one or both parties:

- you're being physically (in any form) mishandled or violated;
- you're told you're "stupid", not wanted or loved by anyone, or not worthy of love;
- you're prevented or blocked from healthy levels of contact with your friends, family and associates; or from forming new friendships that aren't approved of or (therefore) cannot be controlled by the other;
- you're physically isolated so that contact with other people is difficult to achieve;

---

[8] which will come back as a karmic lesson to the one in the wrong anyway, whether they like it or not

- lack of acknowledgment, assistance, encouragement or recognition of/to the abused are commonplace;
- the abuser/controller doesn't permit you to obtain medical treatment when it's clearly necessary or they prevent others from visiting you when you're sick and need company, love, support etc.;
- little or no remorse or regret is shown for harm done;
- the abuser is undoubtedly the 'taker and waiter' not the 'giver and the doer' in the relationship;
- the abuser and abused can role-swap quite easily, when the learned negative behaviors become commonplace in the relationship e.g. in a long term marriage where there's frequent contact between the two parties;
- over time the abused seeks more and more control for themselves, especially as a result of the abuser being non-responsive and non-communicative;
- the abuser is never or rarely there when the proverbial really hits the fan. The abused is left abandoned, repeatedly (including where the abuser sees their having abandoned as "building character" in the abused);
- the children in the family are *very* tightly controlled, monitored, shielded – their life is strictly regimented; have been subjected to physical abuse and no medical attention sought for them; are subjected to high levels of interrogation[9] as to their whereabouts and activities, associates/friends and plans;
- the abuser wants visibility of everything to do with the other and, on the flipside, keeps things close to their chest because they believe that holding information is a more powerful place to be;
- you are discouraged or forbidden from remaining in contact with mutual friends after the relationship has ended;
- a sense of dependency is sought by the abuser through their inference that the abused has no-one else to lean on or talk to other than the abuser;
- over-protectiveness, jealousy, suspicion, back-handed comments, distrust, criticism, disrespect and/or cynicism are commonplace;
- you see the patterns of errors repeating through the generations;

---

[9] as distinct from simple dialogue that demonstrates interest in the other person's life

- you're privately or publicly ridiculed, slandered or discredited in other ways when there's no justifiable reason to do so;
- the abuser/controller portrays themselves as the victim, constantly and most often to save face in public or gain unwarranted sympathy;
- the abuser/controller won't readily let you go, but turns the situation around so that you're portrayed as the one not letting them go; he/she uses emotive questions like "how can I live without you?" or threatens suicide to make you stay;
- in relation to the other, you feel like they're a "noose around my neck" or you're walking on eggshells all the time to avoid upsetting them;
- the abuser/controller accuses you of being "too strong" or, when you defend yourself by getting annoyed at and/or communicate dissatisfaction to the abuser, the abuser then concludes that you're disturbed, troubled or otherwise in need of psychological counselling (perpetuating the myth that the abused is the one in the wrong – that it's all in their head; and not the abuser's fault);
- the abuser will deliberately seek ways to make you cry or upset and then flip to a nurturing, caring role – so the 'emotional healer' dependency (on the abuser) is maintained in the relationship;
- the abuser tells blatant lies to paint a false picture of the abused;
- the abuser/manipulator defends their actions or inactions with a different reasoning each time;
- the abuser repeatedly denies saying what they've said or what they've said suddenly gets turned around as something you've said – deflecting the blame onto you;
- the abuser rarely says sorry, if ever;
- the relationship becomes one of co-dependency, where one or both parties need(s) constant ego-feeding or emotional reinforcement[10] or it becomes emotionally draining to be in contact (i.e. the other partner is high maintenance or too demanding) – refer *No Boxing Allowed* Part 1, Chapter 9 for more about *suckers* and *dumpers*;

---

[10] noting of course that the need for emotional reinforcement can come from not receiving enough support or love from the people who should be giving that to you i.e. an abusive partner may use emotional deprivation and isolation as a means of controlling you

- it's demanded (or requested using dishonorable means) that the abused not speak in their own or another person's defense;
- the abuser accuses you of being needy when you know full well you're not – the abuser actually remains on their power trip whilst ever you're in the vicinity or having contact;
- you plead to be released from any further contact, the abuser then punishes you for wanting out, may even quietly or openly seek revenge, or simply hold and/or express anger that you've left or are planning to leave;
- when you're the abused (having assessed further risk to yourself is too great and thus decided to remain silent for your own wellbeing and sense of self-control) you're then disempowered by someone else disclosing the circumstances of the abusive relationship. The outcome, whilst seen selfishly by the discloser as 'good' for everyone, may be more catastrophic than anticipated. This outcome could place the abused at an unacceptable risk level; and
- you're belittled by the abuser via unwarranted insult or criticism *at the same time* as the abuser is extolling their own goodness and making out they're perfect (which of course no-one is) and without fault.

This is not an exhaustive list but I trust what I've done is empower you to re-evaluate your choices and that the list opens your eyes more readily to the symptoms of potentially toxic, crippling and even fatal relationships. I don't advocate the ending of relationships as a first course of action. Healthy relationships with our fellow human beings are really essential to sustaining and enriching our lives. What I do want you to do though, is find courage to look at yourself, recognize what you or others may have done or are doing wrong, assess the risks involved with making change, make a decision and then act on that decision. Make sure your motives are right first, then make a decision and stick with it.

When *you choose* to remain a victim of *others' choices* – their words, silence, actions and inactions – you're doing yourself and those who love and care about you a grave disservice. As an adult *no-one* has the right to control you and your outcomes[11]. You are always in control of your outcomes with the choices that you make and your destiny is fulfilled

---

[11] except where your choices have resulted in your committing an offence for which you're being punished; or you're under hospitalization or similar for a given period

through the actioning of choices. It's only under extreme circumstances where grave events happen that are not in your control. Thank God that that is so.

Choosing to stay in a relationship that you recognize is abusive, controlling, manipulative or otherwise destructive is always your choice. But I ask you – why suffer it? You *can* change your circumstances.

—————⌇∿∾∘᠙᠊᠌᠊᠐᠊᠌᠐᠊᠌᠐∿∘————

DON'T SUFFER IT, CHANGE IT

—————⌇∿∾∘᠙᠊᠌᠊᠐᠊᠌᠐᠊᠌᠐∿∘————

Perhaps you lack the confidence to speak up; perhaps you lack a positive mindset and foresee negativity and threat with the making of change; perhaps you haven't worked up the contingency plan to activate on your way out. Whatever the reason you choose to stay in a toxic relationship, or one you know doesn't fulfill you completely, *you are choosing to be a victim.*

Victims of events that are completely out of their control deserve our care, compassion and empathy. There's no doubt about that. However, victims of events and circumstances where they have the power to make change and choose not to, deserve naught. Don't tell me that you're not empowered to build a better life for yourself and your child/children if your husband (or for many men, wife) beats you! There are places to go to get help. There are people who will listen. There are avenues for change. Don't tell me that "all hope is lost".

A positive mental attitude and very strong focus on making constructive change for the betterment of yourself, first and foremost, and your/children (who will naturally reap the benefits of the right changes, even if not noticeable at first), is the *best* step in the right direction.

PART 2

Managing The Change

CHAPTER 1

The Fundamentals of Personal Change Management

Before I assist you down this path to a better future, I draw your attention now to the risks, benefits and methods associated with personal change management that are summarized quite clearly in *No Boxing Allowed*. If you've not read *No Boxing Allowed* I strongly recommend that you do read it now, before continuing with this chapter. It will give you the foundation understanding (and support) for the journey that you're choosing to take with me from here on in.

───────⁓⁓⁓⁓───────

Change at any level requires two fundamental foundation stones – strong decision making and ongoing commitment to achieve the strategic and positive outcomes sought. Personal change *must* be managed at a pace and in a manner that's non-destructive, compassionate, empowering and nurturing. Don't push yourself through change. Let your heart, mind, body and soul work through change at a pace they can all take. Your body will tell you when change is too fast as pain levels will increase under that pressure. When you're pushing too hard in your mental effort you'll feel it in your head. When you act or speak contrary to what feels right for your soul then you'll feel a deep-seated disturbance in your whole body – something you may not be able to pinpoint in one specific location, but it'll be there. Don't ignore the signal of increased pain, or

39

soul disturbance. Rather, work to understand where the signal is really coming from and maintain calm and positive while you transition, no matter how short or long the journey.

There's no amount of pressure that someone else can place on you to change, no amount of inspiring words or visions that you see and hear that will influence you more than what is actually in your own mind. As I explain in Part 1, Chapter 10 of *No Boxing Allowed,* your greatest motivation comes from within. When you make a decision to do something (that you trust will bring the best outcome possible), and sustain the focus and energy yourself, then that outcome will occur. Don't look to others to motivate you, for when they're not around who do you rely on then? You'll always have you, no matter what happens. Look to yourself for the drivers you need to make changes that are necessary. And don't look to others as the ones to manage the change for you. *You* are responsible for your own outcomes; *you* are the one who must take responsibility for your choices; *you* are accountable.

As your liver manages your body, *you* manage your attitudinal and behavioural change, and *you* heal yourself of the pain that you carry. Healing yourself of the root cause(s) of your 'PMS' will take the time that's needed. For me, the change was there within the first month (in 2002), but it wasn't for years that I recognized and accepted what had actually happened. My circumstances, to say the least, were quite extraordinary. There's no way I'd recommend someone take the *emotional exfoliation* journey at the same speed I did back in 2002. In all probability the outcome for me could have been either a lost soul not able to find its path or, for my physical body, death. That's not an extreme risk space I want anyone else to ever be in.

However, for me personal change resulted in a great outcome.......sustainable and true. But, it took a *whole* lot of strength and courage to get there. I believe you're quite capable of deciding on and managing yourself through your personal change journey; you just need to keep holding the faith that the outcomes you seek will be delivered to you when the time is right, *no matter what the barriers, challenges, negatives and setbacks you face.*

———∿∿∘๑ၑ✝๑๏✝๑∘∘∿∿———

An important point I'll emphasize here is the need for women and men who've previously been in abusive, controlling, manipulative or in dysfunctional relationships, to *take time to heal from the past first before stepping forward to another relationship.* It's also important that you gain closure from the past, remove any personal baggage (emotional pain associated with memories) and walk forward into a new relationship with a healthy foundation (and a new sense of awareness) from which to start. There's a greater risk of repeating old mistakes, made by yourself or others, and perpetuating the abuse cycle if you haven't recognized within yourself that the abuse, or control, or manipulation was wrong and must never be repeated.

When children learn behaviors of abuse, control and manipulation from one or both parents, or others in their inner sanctum, they generally take those relationship 'rules' and set them up as the foundation stones for their own relationships in the future. If your family has been dysfunctional, the very best gift you can give to your children is to heal yourself first and then help them to see the errors of your ways *before* they move away from home. They'll be less likely to repeat the same mistakes in their own lives.

It's only a very intuitive and strong child who'll see what's wrong (without any real help from others) and make a conscious decision not to repeat the same mistakes in their own life. You can't rely on your child or children to see beyond what's blatantly wrong with you and *expect* them to make right *your* wrongs. You're responsible to make right the wrongs that you create, to the very best of your ability, not them. The karmic lessons fall to you.

CHAPTER 2

Deep Healing

When I think of all the movies, television programs, plays, musicals, radio programs and written words and how they each deliver a slightly different message about what women need and want, it's no wonder men get confused. It's also no wonder women get frustrated or annoyed when they're *expected* (because of this societal and media indoctrination and programming) to think or act a certain way, and when they *don't* fit that 'box' or 'label' because of their unique life experiences, men get frustrated, annoyed (or worse), quiet, reclusive, bewildered and, in some cases, completely apathetic about the relationship.

Likewise for women, when we're programmed with mixed messages about what men need and want, we can respond in exactly the same way.

Life seems pretty easy when we can put women and men into neat little boxes. But isn't that complicating something that's already easy? What I'm getting at here is the *diversity* of women and men, and their ways of managing situations, *must* be more readily tolerated, rejoiced and encouraged. The more you look to keep a woman or man in a box, or labelled a certain way or hold an expectation that they'll all react the *same* way in completely different situations (so that your own comfort zone of understanding can be maintained without any real effort) the more complicated your life will become. Let go of the boxes, the labels, the assumptions and the expectations. We're all human beings after all – each unique, each special, each with priceless gifts to give to each other and our world.

Because of your unique life journey, the way you respond to things at one time in your life will not necessarily be the same way you respond to a similar event at another time in your life. This is because no event or situation will ever replicate itself exactly. Nothing in the past can ever be repeated – something can be very similar, but will never be EXACTLY as it was in the past. That's why we call it *the past.*

As your understanding and knowledge grows, so too will your repertoire of personal life management skills. Managing change is just another one of the skills in your personal tool box that you can choose to hone, to be the best you can possibly be, or choose to shelve or put in the too-hard-basket. I talk more about the too-hard-basket in *No Boxing Allowed.*

In order for deep healing to take place in women, and their men, a conscious decision must first be made. That's really the most challenging of all of the steps in change management. Deciding you really want to do it, and then sticking to it.

Once you reach that point, and perhaps it might be best to put aside this text until such time as you do, then you're ready to take the journey:

STEP ONE: What you must do first, either on your own (if you're unattached) or together (if you're a couple) is *take a giant step sideways, to an open and receptive mind space*, in order that you can start this journey on a path that'll be much easier to navigate, less rocky and far more rewarding in the long term.

STEP TWO: *Brush your teeth using a manual (non-automated) toothbrush using the opposite hand, to what you'd normally use, until such time as both hand actions achieve a balanced and even outcome for your teeth.* What this will do is rebalance your thinking so that both sides of the brain can deliver the outcome equally as well. It's really simple.........don't laugh........do it, and I guarantee your thinking will be stronger and more balanced as a result.

STEP THREE: *Do things and make decisions based on what feels right in your heart – first and foremost.* Don't let someone else's expectations of you push you into a space that doesn't feel right in your heart. When you push your heart too hard or for too long, your soul suffers.

STEP FOUR: *Hold this new truth in your mind at all times – that women and men fundamentally have the same needs, they're not wired or think differently, and they must be free to change and grow at any time they choose in their life journey.* The more I see women and men perpetuate their comfort zone of understanding (that they've been programmed to believe over time) because they don't want to see any differently, the more I feel sorry for the human race as a whole.

From my own personal and irrefutable experience: when I was in blank tape mode (explained in more depth in *No Boxing Allowed*) and especially in the first 18 months of my mind re-engineering, I spent a lot of time listening to men. I sat a test that was designed to prove that women think differently to men. The laughable result was that I came out completely at the male end of the spectrum. I was supposed to be, according to the test, a man. But I wasn't! I am and always have been a woman. So there goes that nonsense theory!

So what did I do to remedy that situation? Well, I knew my early re-programming that had resulted from spending too much time with men was possibly going to give me a non-holistic and unbalanced outcome in the long run. I thus spent the next few months (around 2004) allocating a little more time listening to women, and less to men, and gradually found the 'thinking' space that felt completely balanced and in sync with my body, heart and soul. The way I think is therefore that of a *human being*, not of a "woman" and certainly not of a "man".

STEP FIVE: *Deliver real forgiveness* when your woman or man makes an honest and unplanned mistake.

STEP SIX: *Support each other through the journey of inner healing,* the way that feels comfortable and loving for you both. Don't force a mode or manner that doesn't feel right for your soul or one that you can easily see is distressing or overly demanding of your partner in life. Be compassionate, always. It's not a sissy thing for a man to demonstrate compassion, nor is it a necessity for women to always talk things through. Make sure you and your partner find the space and manner that feels right within your own self. Don't force anything. This deep healing journey is undoubtedly going to be long, at times impossible to navigate, and very emotionally demanding, but if you really want to see things through to the end (for the best possible outcome) you have to be open to changing your perceptions and also to using other means to reassess relationship dynamics.

STEP SEVEN: *Stop offering a solution or remedy every time someone makes a statement to you.* When people need help or advice they will generally come right out and ask for it. If they don't, and you believe they could benefit from your knowledge or wisdom[12], then at least preface your comment with an apology for offering the unsolicited advice. That will show you respect the other person's right of choice to manage their life the way they see fit. Fundamentally people share their thoughts just to share. There are books out in the marketplace that tell women that men are there to help them solve their problems, and these books also program men to believe that women need problem-solvers, and that's the best way to win a woman's favor and love. That simply is a load of rubbish!

Actively listen to people, hear their statements and, unless you're asked a direct question by them and you have a valid answer, shut your mouth before you attempt to offer a 'fix' or advice.

STEP EIGHT: *Understand that when a woman or man suddenly goes quiet, this isn't necessarily a bad thing.* That can be their way of coping with a situation and when the time is right they'll start communicating again (where humanly possible). If communicating with you is what they feel comfortable to do, they they'll do it *when the time is right.* You must be patient to wait for the right time for dialogue.

If someone doesn't wish to communicate anymore, or is continually absent and silent in your life despite your efforts to

---

[12] and remember, gaining wisdom isn't necessarily a given. In order to really be wise you must first choose to learn your lessons and then *apply* the learnings, re-evaluating the results as you go

maintain contact, then you can draw a pretty safe conclusion that your journey together is done. It'd be time for you to move on. Whether or not you have more to experience together as human beings, only time will tell.

STEP NINE: I need you to make a conscious decision to *never make assumptions about anything ever again.* Assumptions, as my precious son so aptly puts it, "make an ass out of you and me". Someone or everyone ends up wearing egg on their face. The one doing all the assuming is working from a completely non-factual base and what they're actually doing is *imposing their expectations* on you, or a situation, in order to gain or influence an outcome that they or others believe is best.

In relationship terms a simple example is where you assume a person is feeling or thinking something, when they're not. That's not to say that when you say something and it's misinterpreted that it's always the *communicatee's* (the receiver's) error because they misinterpreted what was said. As I explain in *No Boxing Allowed*, effective and truthful communication is fundamentally the *communicator's* job to ensure, but both parties can ask questions to clarify their understanding, and clear up misunderstandings along the way.

Remember too that assumptions do not equal impressions or perceptions. People's perceptions are very real and whether we like it or not, people will believe whatever they choose to believe if it's real enough in their own minds, based on their experience, observations or historical reference (be that truthful or not). They may not know you well at all, but they 'box' you a certain way based on their perceptions of similar situations or people, because that's their only adequate frame of reference.

For example, if your *perception* is that someone is feeling angry (rather than simply annoyed or frustrated), then when they express annoyance, irritation or frustration, you may *perceive* them as being angry. Anger is, as we all know, a very negative energy in the body but for some people anger rarely surfaces and for others, like me, anger is an emotion that's no longer in the repertoire of responses. So making an assumption that someone is angry is rather unfair when you don't have all the facts.

When you've used perception as your only frame of reference – rather than invoked intuition or factual analysis – to draw that conclusion, what you owe the other person is benefit of a doubt and time to show their true colors.

STEP TEN: *Learn and understand the difference between disappointment and baggage.* Disappointment is something we all can experience in life when things don't turn out the way we would have liked. Disappointment is usually short-lived. Baggage on the other hand is the residual pain linked to memories – it may manifest as anger outbursts, caustic and deliberately hurtful criticism, or any number of other negative and destructive uses of personal power. But, it doesn't need to be retained and a conscious decision can be made to let go of baggage for good.

For assistance with Letting Go of The Baggage, I refer you to Part 1, Chapter 9 of *No Boxing Allowed.*

STEP ELEVEN: Understand that *when your woman or man has a memory of an event it doesn't mean they hold baggage associated with it.*

In *No Boxing Allowed* (Part 1, Chapter 9) I explain in detail about letting go of baggage and the need for certain memories to be retained. I also explain about memory erasures. When a trauma has occurred in a relationship the parties involved need to retain those memories of the trauma that are critical, as these memories are essential for the person's ongoing survival, defense and/or happiness. The difficulty arises when one, both or all parties want the other(s) to have forgotten certain things – that would, of course, make their life much easier wouldn't it? But life isn't that easy.......nor should it be in order for you to grow and develop as a human being and contribute to your soul's journey over time.

Men must therefore not seek or push for women to forget stuff simply for convenience, nor must women do the same. As a human being you are entitled to retain your memories as long as they are needed.

STEP TWELVE: *Let go of vanity.*

STEP THIRTEEN: *For women,* don't ever work hard to be like a man. You are a woman, and your successes in life will be as a result of you being just who you are, being happy in your femininity, and not pushing to change your man the way *you* want him to be. *For men,* don't ever work hard to change your woman the way you want her to be OR, more importantly, stifle her growth. When you push too hard for change or even keeping status quo it may well backfire in your face.

STEP FOURTEEN: *Start challenging, within your own mind and with other people, everything you hear and see that places women and men in neat little boxes and gives them tidy little labels.* Challenge each other if you hear the statements "Oh, that's so typical of a man" or "All women are moody", "I'm just a stupid man", "I'm a man and can only do one thing at a time" or "I'm only a woman, what would I know", and so on. You're the one who can help stop perpetuating the lies, myths and exaggerations that are common place in our world – immediately, right now.

STEP FIFTEEN: *Learn and respect that making a woman cry doesn't make you a bigger man.* This behavior actually just confirms how long your journey to maturity still has to run and that you're still a boy in your emotional understanding of relationships. Deliberately upsetting a woman sets you on a backwards path. If she perceives you're doing this for some ego gratification then she won't stick around for long. After all, a mature woman is generally looking for a real man – one who is man enough to be nice, not immature and nasty.

STEP SIXTEEN: *Never use 'PMS' as the excuse for anything.* There's more about this in the next chapter.

STEP SEVENTEEN: *Be yourself, be natural, always.* Forget any pretence. It's by being true to ourselves all the time that we find the best path at each stage in our lives. Pivotal events may become turning points for change, but by staying true to yourself through all these events, growing with the changes (in preference to the opposite), a better result will come.

CHAPTER 3

Erasing the Blame Mentality

Forgiveness of oneself and others is a huge step in our journey to wisdom, but for many of you holding blame is a very convenient choice as it provides justification for your thoughts, actions, inaction and words, now and in the future. Blame looks for a loser, a wrong-doer to point the finger at. But in many situations the wrong-doer may well be the one doing the blaming.

Blame looks for a scapegoat, an 'out'. Blame doesn't look at root causes, and it doesn't seek to identify what went, or is going wrong, so that errors of the past aren't repeated again. Blame is short-lived, usually emotive and highly confrontational. It doesn't look to nurture and restore, it simply looks to perpetuate a wrong. Blame is very easy, requires no effort or reflection, and certainly requires no personal change to take place post-blame.

What a blame mentality does is place you in victim mode, a non-empowered space. If you constantly look for someone else to blame, and take no responsibility for your own part in an event or situation, you'll achieve a LOSE/LOSE outcome. That's not what we're looking for here.

How many times have you, or your man, blamed 'PMS' for your behavior and attitude? How many times have you blamed your man for all that is wrong in your life? Is someone else really responsible for everything that goes wrong in your life? How many times have you wished the past had never happened, that something had never taken place; that words had never been spoken?

Come on, be honest?

Now that you've had that reality check............ let's continue.

In order for you to gain maximum benefit from this change journey, you must let go of the label 'PMS'. It's not:

- the reason for your unhappiness;
- the reason for your mood swings;
- an excuse to hide behind every time you don't want to do or participate in something;
- an excuse to use when you feel like being nasty to your family;
- the cause of your anger;
- an excuse for lack of interest in intimacy; and/or
- an excuse to withdraw from the world and those you love.

Likewise gentlemen, 'PMS' isn't your excuse to find fault with your women folk or confine them to a life that must remain static and unchanging. Each day that we move forward to the future, we have an opportunity to take good things along with us and leave the bad stuff behind. Each day that we keep people focused on the past we're not allowing them to be free, and to grow and achieve new and long-held dreams into the future.

In order for there to be a level foundation from which to grow your relationship into the future (a bit like a foundation concrete slab of a home), blame must never be an ingredient. To place blame in the foundation mix you'll end up with a consistency that crumbles in the end. Replace blame with kindness and compassion and you'll have added the two strongest ingredients for a sound, healthy relationship into the future.

The next key thing is not to set any pre-conceived limits on how your relationship is to grow. Sure, you can set boundaries e.g. a friendship not a sexual relationship, but to set forth into a relationship with set ideas that are intended to limit its growth is actually you taking control of the other person's outcomes. Remember, no adult has the right to control another adult. That's a negative use of personal power.

When you both agree on the goal(s) to achieve together, when you both understand each other's motivation(s) in choosing to be in the relationship, then the path that you walk will be smoother than if you didn't share that information up front.

Transparency and trust in relationships are the other two strong ingredients to ensure a healthy, long-term outcome. But before you can trust you must have truth. Perpetual honesty is the *only way* to achieve lasting trust and respect in any relationship.

CHAPTER 4

Changing Expectations

In *No Boxing Allowed* I teach you how to manage, break free of and/or how not be confined or controlled by the expectations of others. It's important to recognize that there are certain expectations that you will bring into the relationship – how you will both behave, what your attitude(s) to certain things will be, and so on. When we're in long-standing relationships, e.g. marriages that go on for decades, and then we choose a different path in life with a new partner, all havoc can break loose if the past expectations (including the learned behaviors and responses) are brought forward into the new relationship.

The most ideal situation, but not always the most practicable or reasonable one, is to approach the new relationship with no prejudices, fears or doubts. Where you're at in your soul journey will dictate how well you can exit and refresh from the old, before taking on the new. But with any journey, seeing it as an adventure – one that will bring new learning, fun, happiness and a sense of fulfilment – will help you to keep the momentum when the going gets harder than anticipated, or when you meet obstacles that have to be removed.

One of the most important things I raise in *No Boxing Allowed* is that the way you are right now is quite OK for you. And likewise for those in a relationship already the way your man is, is quite OK too. When you approach each other with the consistent attitude of "I'm OK, you're OK" you'll find the change phases that much easier to journey through.

Remember too that you'll both journey at different paces. If your man is helping you through the deep healing associated with past pain, helping you to remove the baggage, then he won't necessarily be changing at the same time. In fact he may not need to change at all. He might already be very flexible and adaptable in his approach to life and quite easily able to support you in your healing and changes. You may journey to a different place and then see him somewhere off to the side, out of context to where you are. That's OK too; you'll find your way back to the right spot when that's the best mutually beneficial outcome or at the right time.

You have to trust that the change journey will place you both in a strange/unfamiliar, unpredictable space sometimes. Keep talking together (where possible and mutually agreed) and then the changes won't be quite so dramatic and/or traumatic to deal with.

Ongoing dialogue is critical to sustaining any relationship into the future. Without communication no real growth can occur in a relationship. And it's for this reason that I encourage you to stop believing what we have been wrongly fed for years – that men aren't great communicators; that women are the ones who must do all the talking.

What that nonsense notion does is not only support unnecessary communication, i.e. the filling of quiet with noise, it also allows communication by men to be stifled and controlled. It's an externally imposed expectation that men and women must communicate in different ways, when in reality *we all communicate in the same fundamental way*; we just communicate at different times and with different skill and motivation.

56

WE ALL COMMUNICATE IN THE SAME FUNDAMENTAL WAY; WE JUST COMMUNICATE AT DIFFERENT TIMES AND WITH DIFFERENT SKILL AND MOTIVATION

As you will likely have gathered by now, I'm completely unimpressed with literature that stifles openness, creativity, growth, communication, kindness, peace and compassion in relationships between men and women. The only suggestion that I make to you now is to be careful what you take on board as truth, for there are many falsities propelled in books and over the airways that are designed to deliver cheeky (but of course "scientifically proven") theories simply to make loads of money.

The authors may not care in the slightest what strategic (long term and holistic) impact they'll have on the human race and our inter-relationships. They simply want to pump something gimmicky out into the marketplace for all the wrong reasons.

Be discerning in what you read and hear, form judgments in your mind as to what is true for you, and then follow your instinct about what to put into action. When you place too high an expectation on yourself or your loved one, as can result from following the advice of many 'quick hit' relationship books, things will undoubtedly falter somewhere along the path of change. What you must do is put aside the majority of your existing expectations, holding true to the ones you both agree to as being fair, and then simply go with the flow.

'Going with the flow' is all about knowing that the journey you are on has you in a safe space, you must see that there are only positive outcomes to be achieved, and you must feel empowered to journey at your own pace.

CHAPTER 5

Living Life With Love and Without Force

From my observations of others, my own experience in love-based relationships (including de-facto and legal marriage partnerships) and my experience in relationships with family and friends, the words that come to mind to illustrate the most critical aspect in the success of personal relationships, are *power* and *balance*.

Achieving balance is like walking a fine line at times, a bit like a trapeze high wire. Our relationships may be constantly confronted with disappointments, misunderstandings, losses and betrayals *at the same time* as we're managing major wins and successes, achieving clarity of thinking and action, realizing personal growth and simplifying life. No wonder it's challenging to find balance. While our bodies work to maintain homeostasis, our hearts and minds are working overtime to keep decision-making and risk management as accurate as possible.

Without a more rounded understanding of our own personal power and how to use that more effectively to achieve a WIN/WIN, *and our partner doing the same*, the less easily we'll manage any imbalance. The more out of balance the relationship, the more unequal the expectations, and/or the more determined one is to have power over the other, the rockier the outcome will be.

Personal power, when used wisely and to the best of our ability (without underhanded motives and hidden agendas), will not always give us what we want, but it will open our eyes to a different way of relating.

Whilst ever you feel that your partner, or potential partner, is manipulating an outcome that's not of mutual benefit, or things are done in a way that's not open and transparent, then the negative forces will work against you to achieve the outcome sought. In *No Boxing Allowed* you'll learn much more about your personal power, how to recognize and harness it, the difference between negative and positive power, and how you can change your use of personal power for the benefit of others.

Living a life without force is not about being airy fairy and non-decisive. It's about choosing to remove those factors which create a negative imbalance, or in some cases the actual people who create the negative karmic undercurrents, and choosing to live a simple and uncomplicated life where relationships are easy and unforced.

To get to this point you must have spent time getting to know a person. You can't possibly expect to know someone through written words alone. Feeling a person's energy, being around them and observing, knowing (not just perceiving) how they are and will be in different scenarios, are all part of getting to know them. You can't truly get to know someone in isolation from them. And as they grow and change in their journey and you haven't been there to see the changes first hand, how on earth can you say that you know them at all?

The simplest analogy that I can draw here is where an adult child meets their biological parent for the first time since childhood separation. Often times traumatic, this situation also provides the perfect opportunity to work from that initial foundation, using strong intuition as the guide and taking things at a pace both can tolerate. When couples part and then come back together years later, what do they use as a foundation going forward? They use the good memories, leave the past hurt behind and work from that first encounter (however long ago) as the building block for the future. I've seen that work many times, quite successfully, and it's always the foundation of friendship, trust and caring that helps them achieve the coming together at a time in the future that is right.

Living life with love and without force is about being compassionate and caring towards the person you are with. Living with force, with hidden agendas, or looking for ways to disempower the other will only lead you down a destructive path. Is that what you really want?

The most effective use of personal power in a relationship is therefore one where energies feel equal, no-one feels disempowered or disadvantaged, a WIN/WIN has taken place, both parties live together without force and with loving undercurrents.

Living life with love and trust, and without any kind of power imbalance, is the foundation stone critical to a mutually rewarding, long-term relationship.

CHAPTER 6

The Armory

I love many things in life but, of all, I love hearing a woman talk about nurturing herself, giving to herself, pampering herself – simple, no fuss, low cost, soul nourishing ways such as:

- taking time out for self-awareness and enjoyment;
- rewarding herself with little things that bring pleasure;
- spending time with people who enrich her sense of worth;
- reflecting; or simply
- languishing in her thoughts, dreams and plans.

Ah, how simple, uncomplicated and positive life is when we give to our own self!

It's my wish that every woman (and man) who reads this book, re-evaluates just how vital it is to love oneself. I don't mean the egotistical, selfish self-love. I mean the soul nurturing, self-acceptance kind of love that only comes when you give yourself time to really get to know yourself, to understand what your soul needs.

When a woman *really* knows herself she's generally more equipped to teach a man what she needs, but this will *only* be successful if the man is open and receptive to that learning. He must be as in tune with her as he is with himself. So .... what I'm really saying here is that the man has to practice and refine the nurturing, pampering and giving to *himself* too! And of course *he* will then be more able to teach *her* what he needs!

Feeding yourself your own good, positive energy is not just a woman's entitlement; it's everyone's.

———————————

For much of my life, being a giver by nature not a taker, I rarely (and can probably only count on both hands) gave anything of real significance to myself. It took me decades to realize that it was OK to spend time having long hot baths soaking in perfumed bubbles; to go for long, healthy and invigorating walks; to open a bottle of wine, grab some nibblies and crackers and just *enjoy*; to sit for hours watching movies or TV shows of interest; to hand knit special gifts for people hour after hour without moving (where previously I had grabbed an hour here and there in between rushing around for others); to walk around outside at home and just 'smell the roses' and enjoy nature in every way.

I never had any hesitation spending time with family, gardening, playing sports, fishing, holidaying and so on (these are all good for my soul), but when it came time to so something that was special *just for me*, I always felt guilty that I wasn't doing for others – and so many women I know and hear of, think and act the same way I did.

But, do you know what? The easiest and most empowering thing to do to fix this imbalance is simply to make the decision to change! As hard as you might think that is, as much as you feel you'd be betraying your family and not honoring your responsibilities, my sense is that it will be the *best* decision you ever make. And, what will most likely happen is you will see others follow your lead when they see the benefits that change and self-giving have done for you.

———————————

Only you will know, deep inside, what really nurtures you at a holistic whole-of-person level; what feels best (all over) when you're giving to yourself. Only you'll know whether what you do brings physical, mental, emotional and/or spiritual fulfilment and enjoyment. Go with the flow in the choices you make. Spend minimal time questioning and procrastinating. Stay in the moment; for it's staying in the moment with yourself, tapping into your essence and using every sense you have to learn what you need, that you'll rise to an entirely different and, most likely, euphoric level of understanding.

Trust yourself that you'll know your own boundaries. Trust yourself that, once self-educated, you'll then be able to teach others what you need and where the boundaries are that must never be crossed.

So what are the ways to give to ourselves? Well the list below, whilst not exhaustive, is a start. These are some of the common, well understood, trusted and pretty much fool-proof ways. Some may not be your cup of tea right away, some may take you right out of your comfort zone the first time (e.g. massage), but once you have a go at them I'd be surprised if you didn't become a convert for life!

Massage (Swedish, therapeutic, remedial/sports, deep tissue, lymphatic drainage, reflexology-based etc. – whichever is your choice):

First and foremost massage must be delivered by a trained, accredited and appropriately skilled therapist otherwise considerable damage can be done to superficial and deep blood vessels, the musculoskeletal structure, and the heart/mind/soul. A massage therapist is in your personal space, in your aura, so how that person's energy matches with yours is vital to the success of the massage. If the energy that you're receiving during massage just doesn't feel right, then stop.

Despite the innumerable positive benefits, any massage undertaken for the first time or after a long period of absence could trigger a number of flow-on effects – skin eruptions, increased digestive tract activity, increased bowel movements, tiredness (due mainly to flooding into the lymphatic system of toxins previously trapped in muscle cells – now released by massage and manipulation), emotional hypersensitivity for a short time afterwards, headache, muscle or tissue pain or tenderness, or even increased redness of massaged areas. All likely flow-on effects from the type of massage therapy you undertake *must* be explained to you by the therapist. If you don't have the explanation offered to you then ask *before* you leave the session. For some people, especially those receiving deep tissue or drainage-type therapies, the after effects can be *so* different to their expectations this in turn can raise a person's physical body stress levels which may then negate any positives delivered by the massage in the first place.

There's another important point that I want to emphasize here as well:

After I trained as a remedial massage therapist I went on to become an Internationally Accredited Infant Massage Instructor. I still have the equipment and teaching materials I used when I was conducting classes for moms, dads, grandparents and their bubs, and teaching/delivering massage is still one of my greatest joys in life. But of all the things I learned over the years of study and refinement of my skills, it was knowing and teaching the difference between right and wrong touch. Touch, especially for someone who is blind, is *the* most powerful sensory input for the soul. It's through touch that we know someone's energy; it's by touching that we understand our own power. To use touch wisely we do great benefit to others. To touch wrongly, or with force, we can do great harm. Consider that for a moment; and when you are receiving massage from another person always follow your instinct when it comes to what feels right, and what feels wrong.

Yoga / Pilates / Tai Chi:

I could write for hours about how wonderful these are, but you really must experience them for yourself to see just how powerful and positive they are in strengthening not only your body but your mind. Imagine for a moment that your navel is the center of the universe; imagine that your body has the ability to bend, turn, hold itself, extend and lengthen beyond any previous range of limited motion. That's the potential, within your own physiological limits of course, that yoga and Pilates and tai chi can deliver to you every day as often as you need. All are slow, energy-building, grounding/earthing, stabilizing, toning and strengthening activities. They'll take time for you to understand the true value of and to master. But, most importantly, once you know their beauty and power they'll be with you (in your armory) for life.

Exercise:

How many of you say to yourselves "I'll start exercising tomorrow" and then when tomorrow comes, it becomes the next day, and then the next day. Too often we find excuses for putting off something which can be fun as well as good for us. Whatever the exercise you do there are some core things to remember:
- follow an exercise regime that suits you as an individual - your body, age, fitness level, budget and so on;
- exercise within your pain tolerance - never exceed this;
- do what's fun;
- do it as often as you have available time;
- exercise during all kinds of weather, but without putting your health at risk of course;

66

- learn to exercise alone so that you become self-motivated and don't rely on others to keep you going;
- make it a family activity that everyone can enjoy, if this is a more practicable solution;
- forget the expensive exercise gear – wear what feels comfortable; and
- treat yourself to something special when you've achieved a fitness goal that you're proud of.

Nutrition:

In *No Boxing Allowed* I explain about how important it is to maintain appropriate nutrients levels in order for the brain to function properly and send the correct messages to the body. We all know that processed food generally is less nutritious, that fresh food is better. Best still is fresh food that comes from trusted sources (home grown fruit and vegetables, freshly caught seafood, local market meats and eggs, and so on).

Remember though that our nutritional intake each day, and its utilization by the body, is subject to a number of factors related to how our bodies assimilate nutrients and distribute what's needed to every cell in the body. The better the quality of nutrients, the more chance you give the body to manage itself well. Our bodies are remarkable in their ability to repair themselves and restore imbalances. Feeding yourself a well-rounded diet of foods and liquids that sustain life to the optimal degree also gives you the best chance at longevity to a ripe and healthy old age. Our *biological potential* is greater than 135 years (based on evidence presented at the first International Longevity Conference in 2004), so really middle age is not reached until you're around 67.5 years old. Therefore, when does "old age" really start?

Eat well, live life well, put fun and life into ageing and you too have the potential to live way beyond your life expectancy 'box'.

Rest / Relaxation:

These two items in the armory are pretty much self-explanatory, however they're the ones least likely to be on the top of your list. Right?

When you reflect back on the case study ladies, one of them talked about how the pace of Western living has a lot to do with a woman's ability to rest and relax from the daily grind of things. So too, it's important that men rest and relax. Each of us will do these things in our own way, but it's essential that we do actually do them. The 'I'm too stressed to relax' mindset must be eliminated and replaced with inner dialogue that says something like "I'm going to relax now. Take time out for me. It's important that I get to rest when my body says so. I'm going to listen to my body and when it says take it easy, that's just what I'll do." Keep feeding yourself approval-to-rest messages and your body will get in sync accordingly. Always remember the mind-body connection, the 'you are what you think' mindset.

There's absolutely no karmic wrong, shame or mistake in resting when you need. Whatever the reason to rest, do it when your body says it needs it, or as soon as possible thereafter, so that you give yourself the best outcome (e.g. rejuvenation and recovery) possible.

Ongoing Emotional Cleansing (Exfoliation):

What I advocate in this book is the beginning, the middle and the end of a whole new way of life for you and your man. Changes that you choose to make will occur in you at a rate that feels best and is most manageable. Never push yourself through change, especially at an emotional level. Never change to fit another person's image for that would not truly be you, would it?

No matter how easy it sometimes is to fall back to old coping mechanisms when you've been hurt, as much as the habits and patterns that you've developed and/or been programmed with over time are hard to break, you must hold faith that new ways of living and loving can be achieved by simply hanging in there and thinking new empowering and self-loving thoughts. Have faith in yourself, each other, and those who really love you, for it is they who will help you get through any future challenges.

No matter what the cause of your emotional pain, you don't have to hold onto it. Practice makes perfect – you may have heard that saying at some stage in your life – so practice the emotional exfoliation techniques you find here and in *No Boxing Allowed*, to give yourself the *best* possible chance to live a life that is pain free, blissful and content.

———

Last of all I'd like you to consider this option in your armory:

Knowing the Reality of Living Alone and that Alone ≠ Lonely:

Successfully living on your own and being self-sufficient requires a high level of strength and the more strenuous the circumstances the greater the strength required. It requires courage, confidence, patience, a sense of humor (mainly about yourself), resourcefulness, creativity, innovative thinking, and a high level of self-control to live alone without faltering. And there are times when living alone can present huge challenges and sometimes quite grave risks e.g. when you're sick or have an injury. Who do you turn to when there's no-one around? You always have to have a contingency but, more importantly, you have to keep yourself as safe as possible all the time. That way you're not risking your life or inconveniencing anyone else unnecessarily.

The most obvious difficulty that can arise is when you've been in a relationship for any length of time and then suddenly you find yourself on your own. All of the things that you've learned to share with someone else, all the difficulties in life that you've had someone to talk to about, cannot be done like that now.

Living alone you learn, by necessity, to find a level of resourcefulness within and build alternate ways to share with others.

When it all boils down to it, our choices in life usually come as a result of the facts that present at the time, an intuitive feel for what needs to be done, our perception of what is happening around us and/or the findings that come from searching our soul for answers. For you to know the reality of living alone, and that being alone doesn't equal lonely, you'll be better placed to understand the joy of sharing life with someone else when the time is right. And always remember that whether you choose to live alone or together *that choice at that time is the right choice* for you.

PART 3

The Ultimate Gift to Yourself and Your Loved Ones

CHAPTER 1

Valuing Yourself and Others

When you think about personal value do you automatically think of dollar value?

The reason I ask this is because quite a few years back a male colleague made a comment to me about people being a commodity, with a certain dollar value, and that we must never sell ourselves short. I'd never heard people referred to as a commodity[13] and, to a certain extent, I was disappointed that he thought that way. But, more importantly, that any human being could be seen as such. As disappointed as I was it was clear that perhaps that's the way some people choose to measure one person's value against the next.

What's important to remember is that every human being is special, unique and valuable, not for what they're worth in dollar terms, but for what they bring to humanity and our world. Every human being has something great to give to others and our universe, *if they choose to.*

Life is full of choices and we generally do the best we can each day to make decisions and choices based on the facts we have available. Sometimes the choices we make are very hard, sometimes they're easy, but the key to making choices is doing so based on what feels right and true in your heart. When you heart is hurting then the choices can be difficult to tolerate because of the disturbance that's created. However, as the dust clears and you achieve clarity through reflection or fact finding/checking, the strategic correctness of your choices will be validated.

---

[13] other than in the context of slavery or being bought and sold to provide a service

The most valuable gift you can give yourself is to really *value yourself 100%*. No-one is perfect and so often women work hard to be perfect every day. It's important to understand that you can still be the best you can be every day, but fall way short of perfect! After all, achieving perfection means you require no further refinement and you have no more lessons to learn. Your soul will have reached the end of its journey to perfection and not need another 'life' through which to grow.

As a human being you are priceless – don't ever forget that. There's no monetary value that could ever be placed on your head that would equal your true worth. So, when you think of your true 'value' we have to look at the non-monetary ways that exhibit this, such as:

- how you treat yourself;
- how you treat others;
- how much you value your contribution to others and to our universe;
- what you give; and
- what you are capable of receiving from others.

The most powerful influencer in terms of recognition of your true value is you! Who else knows you better than you do? No-one can read your mind, feel what's in your heart or measure the depth of your soul. So if you're ever in that space, where you feel and believe you're not being truly valued by others, then make a change. Don't suffer it when others put you down or question your worth! Don't de-value *yourself* just because others choose to devalue you. Step outside of that negative space and realize just how priceless you really are.

REALIZE JUST HOW PRICELESS YOU REALLY ARE

When criticism is unjustified, when negativity is all around you, when you're constantly giving and not receiving, it's time to confront the reality, see it for what it really is and do something about it that's positive.

My former stepson Derek tragically died in a light plane crash in 2005, when he was in his early 30's. As a child he was full of confidence, however as he transitioned through adolescence to early adulthood we had many conversations about an individual's value.

The saddest point was reached (around 1992 when he was 20) when he shared with me that he saw himself as never meeting the expectations of one of his parents (his father), and of never being considered good enough by many people. He asked me then "What if my best just isn't good enough?"

My response to him then was to never undervalue himself as a person or member of our family. The unrealistic expectations of others that we must be and do *better* than our best, that we must deliver 200% effort, not simply 100% (which is our best when all said and done) must never be the indicator of our value.

Derek's value to me can be summed up in these personal and unique ways. He:

- ➢ appreciated my cooking, party hosting and other family contributions;
- ➢ listened when I wanted or needed to talk;
- ➢ watched me cry in pain and never judged me for it;
- ➢ gave time to his brother, my son;
- ➢ gave gifts that are still cherished; and
- ➢ talked to me about things that even his biological parents were not privy to know, sharing his innermost thoughts about a whole range of things and seeking advice where he needed.

I had the priceless gift of his presence in my life, directly and indirectly, for 23 years in all and he, along with his late sister Toni, will always be valued.

CHAPTER 2

The Power of A Positive Mental Attitude

No Boxing Allowed sets the framework and strategies for you in terms of how to recognize where you are in your life journey and whether your mindset is predominantly negative or positive. I explain that, with few exceptions, humans are born positively 'programmed'. Whilst a baby in utero is receiving messages into its subconscious mind, being programmed by what it senses and receives at a spiritual level, there's only a very small percentage of babies who would be receiving 100% negative messages in every context. For them, the journey back to positive is likely to be very challenging. But for the majority of you who've already reached a level of emotional maturity, and understand or have a sense for what your mindset is, the journey to positive will be far less daunting.

When you look around every day, how many people do you see smiling? Few? Many? It varies doesn't it?

In simple terms that's because we all experience different degrees of happiness or positivity every day. A positive person will be more consistent about what they want out of life and how they feel every day. With a positive mental attitude, each day will be faced with happiness and you'll see life through a whole different lens. What made you unhappy 6 months ago may bring joy today. What seemed insurmountable 5 years ago may now be something you reflect on and say "I don't know what the big deal was back then. It all turned out just fine in the end!"

Out of every adversity, out of every worst case situation, *something* of positive value will come. You just need to have a positive mental attitude, that strong mental posture that *No Boxing Allowed* challenges and teaches you to achieve, and look for the positives at *every* opportunity; hold them close and focus on them. Once the negative wave has passed, the light will shine again – perhaps even brighter than before.

Earlier in Part 1 I explained how a negative mindset is actually toxic to me. It causes physiological changes that I can recognize immediately, and each day that goes by the positive reinforcement coming from my subconscious makes the negative thought process 'event' that much easier to identify. What might have taken a few days to see the impact of, I can now identify straight away. What a bonus! It's like a nudge from my soul that says "Snap out of it Nola!" It's instant, it's consistent and, most importantly, it lays yet another positive and strong piece of the frame on top of the positive mental attitude 'slab'.

How you journey through the process of self-realization to that higher level of self-intelligence is yours to determine. How well and how strongly you hold a positive mental attitude about life is also yours to choose. As I also explain in *No Boxing Allowed,* the choice you make in life to move to a positive mindset is a journey that must never be reversed. That journey of discovery, where you'll see the lightness of positivity and the darkness of negativity in stark contrast to each other, will be both challenging and exciting. But without doubt it will be rewarding, not only for you but for your loved ones in your inner sanctum who feel and live right alongside you every day, week and month.

Not only will *you* receive great rewards for living life with a positive mental attitude, so too will your family and friends. For each woman and man to recognize, grow and share the positive during every exchange with each other, the universal rewards will come back tenfold.

As you put out positive karma so too it will return to you tenfold. As you put out negative the return karma will come back double fold in negative intensity each time.

What would you choose?

Ladies – as one of you I know just how hard life can be every second, every minute, every day. But what I can promise you is that when you have fully healed from any emotional pain that you carry, when you have achieved full closure on the past and can retain a positive mental attitude through even the worst adversity, those menstrual cycle pains and other symptoms will be gone for good.

As true as I write these words I know in my heart and soul that you'll then be able to live a life where menstruation and hormonal changes are no more impacting than having to brush your teeth or choose what clothes to wear. You'll finally feel the power of the light and experience the bliss of true happiness and freedom.

Your man may not immediately recognize the gift he's being given by supporting you the way you need through that journey, but at some point along the way he'll probably wake up and say "Hey; wait for me! I'm coming on that journey too."

If your man gave you this book, and especially if he gave you *No Boxing Allowed* as well, it's most likely his way of showing you just how much you mean to him, how much he values what you have together, and how much he believes in you and your ability to succeed in life.

PMS is a thing of the past
– let it go!

PERSONAL NOTES

PERSONAL NOTES

PERSONAL NOTES

PERSONAL NOTES

PERSONAL NOTES

www.ingramcontent.com/pod-product-compliance
Lightning Source LLC
Chambersburg PA
CBHW072152020426
42334CB00018B/1968